Festivals *of the* World

GREECE

Gareth Stevens Publishing
MILWAUKEE

Written by
EFSTATHIA SIORAS

Edited by
GERALDINE MESENAS

Designed by
LOO CHUAN MING

Picture research by
SUSAN JANE MANUEL

First published in North America in 1998 by
Gareth Stevens Publishing
1555 North RiverCenter Drive, Suite 201
Milwaukee, Wisconsin 53212 USA

For a free color catalog describing Gareth
Stevens' list of high-quality books and multimedia
programs, call
1-800-542-2595 (USA)
or 1-800-461-9120 (Canada).
Gareth Stevens Publishing's Fax: (414) 225-0377.
See our catalog, too, on the World Wide Web:
http://gsinc.com

Originated and designed by
Times Books International
an imprint of Times Editions Pte Ltd
Times Centre, 1 New Industrial Road
Singapore 536196
Printed in Singapore

Library of Congress Cataloging-in-Publication Data:
Sioras, Efstathia.
Greece / by Efstathia Sioras.
p. cm.—(Festivals of the world)
Includes bibliographical references and index.
Summary: Describes how the culture of Greece is
reflected in its many festivals, including
Independence Day, Carnival, and Pascha.
ISBN 0-8368-2014-2 (lib. bdg.)
1. Festivals—Greece—Juvenile literature. 2. Fasts
and feasts—Greece—Juvenile literature. 3.
Greece—Religious life and customs—Juvenile
literature. 4. Greece—Social life and customs—
Juvenile literature. [1. Festivals—Greece. 2.
Holidays—Greece. 3. Greece—Social life and
customs.] I. Title. II. Series.
GT4851.A2S56   1998
394.269495—dc21   98-16236

1 2 3 4 5 6 7 8 9 02 01 00 99 98

CONTENTS

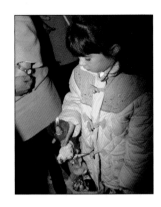

It's Festival Time . . .

The Greek word for festivals is *panigyria* [pa-ni-gee-ri-AH] and they are mostly religious celebrations. Most Greeks follow the Greek Orthodox religion, and each festival is accompanied by a story from the Bible that explains the significance of the festival. Greeks always enjoy their festivals with lots of music, dancing, and traditional food. They are a very hospitable people and love to invite others to celebrate with them. So why don't you come along, too? It's festival time in Greece!

WHERE'S GREECE?

Greece is situated in southeast Europe, in a region that borders the Mediterranean Sea. Other countries in Europe, Africa, and the Middle East also border the sea. This entire region is often referred to generally as the Mediterranean, because the sea washes against their shores.

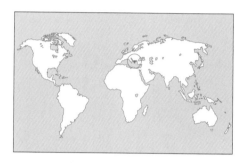

Greece is a very old part of Europe and is more than 4,000 years old. It is a small country—only a little larger than the state of Alabama in the United States. Over 1,400 islands dot the blue waters around the Greek mainland. The capital of Greece is Athens, named after Athena, the goddess of wisdom.

Schoolboys on the island of Crete.

Below: The Porch of the Caryatids in the Acropolis. Built almost 2,500 years ago during the Golden Age in Greece, the Acropolis was actually a fortress built on the highest point of the city of Athens. Its ruins still exist today.

Who are the Greeks?

The Greek people of today are the descendants of all the different tribes and peoples that have invaded and conquered the lands of Greece, such as the Franks, the Turks, and the Venetians. Most Greeks are Christians of the Greek Orthodox faith. Other small groups of Christians in Greece include the Roman Catholics and the Jews.

Greeks are very proud of their ancient **civilization**. In fact, Greek art, architecture, language, literature, music, and religion have greatly influenced the Western world.

WHEN'S THE PANIGYRIA?

Want to learn about how Greece gained its independence? Come visit me at Constitution Square on page 10.

WINTER

✪ **CHRISTMAS**—The day is celebrated with fasting, church services, and big family meals. Nativity scenes dot the main cities and towns. Children traditionally wait until New Year's Eve to open their presents.

✪ **NEW YEAR'S DAY**—Families gather after church to cut the New Year cake. Every member of the family receives a piece, even members who have passed away. The Greeks believe that the one who finds the foil-wrapped coin in their piece of cake will enjoy extra good luck that year.

✪ **EPIPHANY**—This is a very old Christian tradition. On January 6th every year, hundreds of Greeks gather at the nearest port, river, or lake, for the blessing of the waters by a priest.

SPRING

✪ **INDEPENDENCE DAY**
✪ **CARNIVAL**
✪ **EASTER**
✪ **ST. GEORGE'S DAY**—St. George is the patron saint of Greece and of shepherds. Families spend the day visiting relatives in the countryside.
✪ **MAY DAY**—To celebrate spring, wild flowers are woven into wreaths and hung as decorations on the doors of houses.
✪ **ANASTENARIA (FIRE-WALKING FESTIVAL)**—Some Macedonian villages celebrate the fire-walking ritual, which occurs every year on May 21st, the feast day of St. Constantine and St. Helen.

6

SUMMER

- ✪ **PENTECOST OR WHIT SUNDAY**— Celebrated seven weeks after Easter, this is a very important feast day in the Greek Orthodox church.
- ✪ **FEAST OF ST. JOHN THE BAPTIST**— On this day, everyone named John celebrates, and the wreaths from May Day are burned in bonfires.
- ✪ **ASSUMPTION OF THE VIRGIN MARY**

AUTUMN

- ✪ **BIRTH OF THE VIRGIN MARY**—An important feast day in the Orthodox church, Greeks throughout Greece celebrate the birth of Mary, the mother of Jesus.
- ✪ **ST. DIMITRIOS' DAY**—St. Dimitrios is the patron saint of Thessaloniki, the second largest city in Greece. Families roast lambs on a spit and perform traditional dances to folk music.
- ✪ **OCHI DAY**—In 1940, when the Italian prime minister, Mussolini, asked for the surrender of Greece, the Greek prime minister at that time, Metaxas, replied with a forceful "No!"(*ochi* in Greek). This day commemorates Metaxas's famous reply. The Greeks celebrate this day with parades, music, and dancing.

INDEPENDENCE DAY

On March 25th every year, the Greeks celebrate the 1821 revolt against the Ottoman empire. This is a national holiday, with parades and dances nationwide. On this special day, schoolchildren dress up in white shirts and blue skirts and pants (which are the colors of the Greek flag) and march in parades from their schools to the town square.

Above: The Greek flag is made up of two colors—blue and white. These two colors reflect the two strongest colors of the Greek landscape: the blue of the sea and the white of the rocky landscape.

In the parade

The lucky child selected to head the parade carries a large Greek flag. Children line up in neat rows and listen while the mayor, or another important person, gives a speech, reminding everyone of the historic struggle to gain independence and the heroes of that time. Several children are also chosen to read poems, after which everyone sings the national anthem. After the parade, families gather at local cafes to enjoy coffee and cakes and to chat with friends.

Left: Two boys in national dress on Independence Day.

Bishop Germanos and Greek independence

Above: Greek-Americans in the U.S. city of Chicago celebrate the Greek Independence Day. The United States has one of the largest Greek populations outside Greece.

For almost 400 years, Greece was ruled by the Ottoman Turks. This was a long, dark period in Greek history, when Greeks struggled to keep their traditions, religion, and language alive.

On March 25th, 1821, Archbishop Germanos of Patrai raised the Greek flag at the Monastery of Agias Lavras in the Peloponnese, which is situated in the southern peninsula of Greece. This act of **defiance** inspired Greeks throughout the country, who started to fight against their Turkish **oppressors**. Both sides fought ferociously, and it took eight years before the Ottoman Sultan (the ruler of the Ottomans) recognized Greek independence.

Right: The Monastery of Agias Lavras in the Peloponnese.

Above: The Tomb of the Unknown Soldier on the front of the Parliament House. The Tomb is decorated with a sculpture of a dying Greek warrior and was unveiled on March 25th, 1932.

The Greek Constitution

In the heart of the city of Athens is Constitution Square. Although Greeks celebrate Independence Day on March 25th, Greece actually became an independent nation on September 3rd, 1843. On this day, King Otto, who ruled Greece from 1832 to 1862, stood on the balcony of the Royal Palace in Constitution Square and presented the constitution to the people. A constitution is a written set of rules stating how a country is to be governed responsibly and justly. The Royal Palace later became the Parliament House, and Constitution Square continues to be a place where rallies and parades take place.

Right: Greek soldiers stand guard in front of Parliament House every day of the year. These are special guards called *evzones* [EV-zones]. These guards traditionally came from the Macedonian village of Evzone. Their uniform of fitted jacket, full short skirt, stockings with **tassels** at the knees, and clogs decorated with pom-poms is similar to that worn by the *klephts* [KLEFTS]. Klephts were mountain fighters who fought **valiantly** in the War of Independence.

Ochi Day

In World War II, many countries lost their freedom. The leader of the Greeks at that time, Ioannis Metaxas, wanted his country to remain **neutral** so Greece could keep its independence. When Italy, which supported the Germans, wanted Italian troops to enter Greece, Metaxas did a very brave thing. He replied with a single word—*ochi* [o-HEE], meaning "no." Although German troops eventually invaded Greece, Metaxas's famous response is remembered by Greeks on October 28th every year.

Ochi Day is celebrated with music, dancing, and military parades where the colors of the Greek flag flutter in the wind. Memorial services are also held for those who died in the country's struggle for independence.

The Memorial Chapel in the Monastery of Agias Lavras. It commemorates the day in 1943 when the Germans set fire to the town of Kalavryta—4 miles (6 kilometers) from the monastery—and massacred 1,436 men and boys for resisting them. The cathedral clock is permanently stopped at the time the killing started.

Think about this
March 25th is also the day of a religious festival, the Feast of the Annunciation. The Annunciation refers to a story in the Bible when the angel Gabriel visited Mary to tell her that she was going to give birth to Jesus, the son of God.

CARNIVAL

Carnival season takes place over the three weeks before Lent. Carnival is all about fun and enjoyment, dancing, music, and games. There are parades and costume balls in many large cities. During this period, many big carnivals take place all over Greece. The most elaborate and **exuberant** celebrations take place in Skiros, one of the Sporades Islands in the Aegean Sea, and Patrai, a city on the Peloponnese peninsula.

Skiros Carnival

The island of Skiros has a wealth of history and legend surrounding it and was a center of the sea trade for thousands of years. During Carnival season, Skirians celebrate with lots of food, music, and dancing, as well as poetry readings and theatrical performances. The famous feature of the Skiros Carnival is the goat dance.

A young goat dancer at the Skiros Carnival.

The goat dance

Skiros's famous goat dance is one of the few rites in Greece that originated from **pagan** festivals. It occurs on the last two Sundays before Clean Monday, the first Monday in Lent, and is the highlight of the Skiros Carnival.

Groups of young men in masks and costumes parade through the narrow streets of Skiros town, making lots of noise. At the center of these groups are young men dressed up in goat masks, hairy jackets based on the traditional shepherd's outfit, and lots of noisy copper goat bells that hang from their costumes. The goat dancer is called the *geros* [YEE-ros], meaning "old man." The dancers walk through town, jumping around so the bells ring continuously.

Above: Goat dancers in the Skiros Carnival. Notice the goat masks on the dancers' faces and the big copper bells around their waists.

Below: Little children in colorful costumes in the Skiros Carnival, accompanied by their parents.

The Patrai Carnival

The most famous Greek Carnival takes place in a city called Patrai on the Peloponnese peninsula. The Patrai Carnival has a very long tradition. It is part of the identity of the townspeople of Patrai.

In the main streets of the town, the Carnival begins with the *telalis* [te-LA-lis], or public announcer, walking through the main streets, loudly announcing the upcoming events. Carnival tunes are played in the streets, while people stand on their balconies, clapping and cheering. The opening procession involves a special game for children called The Hidden Treasure Hunt. The three weeks that follow are filled with all kinds of fun activities and events, such as mask-making, theater performances, children's bicycle contests, dances, a custard pie contest, and many more.

The big parade is one of the highlights of the Carnival. There are hundreds of floats, with all sorts of themes. Many children take part in the parade.

Above: All sorts of costumes and masks can be seen in the Carnival parade—from the funny to the **grotesque**.

Think about this

Many countries in the world celebrate the Carnival season for all sorts of reasons. Some, like the Greek Carnival, are celebrated for religious reasons. Have you been to a Carnival before? Were there lots of people in costumes and masks?

King Carnival

The night after the parade is a special time. This is when the statue of King Carnival is burned on the harbor, with fireworks lighting up the sky behind. On the last night of the Carnival, people feast and celebrate throughout the night for the last time before the beginning of Lent and fasting.

Right: Children dressed up in Carnival costumes.

PASCHA

Pascha [PAS-cha], which means "Easter" in Greek, is the most important religious festival for Greeks. Its focus is Easter Sunday, a date that changes slightly from year to year. Pascha is celebrated on the last day of Holy Week, which occurs during the last week of Lent—a time of fasting and **repentance**. During Lent, many Greeks will not consume meat, olive oil, and alcohol.

Opposite: The Niptras [nip-TRAS] (washing) ceremony on Maundy Thursday before Good Friday. On this day, hundreds of people pack the town of Chora in Patmos to watch the ceremony. The abbot of the Monastery of St. John publicly washes the feet of 12 monks, reenacting Christ's washing of His disciples' feet before the Last Supper.

Below: Boys in the Easter procession on Easter Sunday.

Pascha

Pascha celebrates the crucifixion of Jesus Christ (Jesus was nailed to a cross at His hands and feet, and He died) and His resurrection (this means He came back to life) three days later . Although He died such a horrible death, Greeks see Easter as a joyous event because He came back to life.

Left: Easter bread and biscuits are eaten to celebrate the end of Lent.

Megali Paraskevi

The festival begins in earnest on Megali Paraskevi [Me-GA-li Pa-ras-ke-VI], which is Good Friday. Women and girls gather in the local church and spend the day decorating the bier (an open container representing Jesus' coffin) with flowers. In the past, only red and white flowers were used, but, today, flowers of all colors are used to make a colorful display.

On the evening of Good Friday, everyone gathers in the church for the long procession through the streets. The priest slowly walks out of the church, closely followed by several people carrying the bier on their shoulders. Everyone holds a lighted candle, and the long procession through the neighborhood begins. The procession makes several stops along the way at the Seven Stations of the Cross, which depict Christ's suffering before His crucifixion. At these stops, the priest reads gospel verses relating Christ's suffering and leads the people in prayer.

Right: The church procession on Good Friday. This is a day of total fasting as the people remember Christ's suffering and His sacrifice on the cross.

Christ is risen

On Saturday night, everyone stays up late and gathers at their local church close to midnight. Just before midnight, all the lights of the church are turned off and everyone stands silently in the darkness, representing Jesus' passage through the **realm** of death. As midnight passes, the priest lights the first candle, and, ever so slowly, the light moves through the church as everyone's candle is lit. Soon the church is softly glowing with light. People turn to one another and say, "*Christos anesti*" [Chri-STOS a-NE-sti], meaning "Christ is risen," and others respond, "*Alithos*" [Ali-THOS], meaning "Truly He is risen." Fireworks are set off, and people return home to a big celebration and feasting.

Above: Easter decorations in Rhodes depict the Seven Stations of the Cross.

Below: Red-dyed eggs are a special part of Easter. The egg represents new life. Friends and family carefully choose one egg on Easter Sunday. The tradition is to crack the top or bottom of your egg against someone else's egg. If your egg is not broken, you will have a lucky year.

Think about this

Easter is the most important festival for the Greek Orthodox Church. The people celebrate their belief that Christ comes to life during Easter. Who is the central figure in other religions?

ASSUMPTION OF THE VIRGIN MARY

On August 15th, all Greeks celebrate the assumption of Mary into heaven. It is one of the most important festivals in the Greek Orthodox Church. It is a happy event and a special day for everyone named Mary or Maria.

Right: A Byzantine-style silver icon of the Virgin Mary and the Infant Jesus.

Listen to a story

Below: A girl during the festival of the Assumption of the Virgin Mary celebration in the town of Karpathos.

The Bible tells the story of Mary, who gave birth to Jesus, the son of God. Mary is known as the mother of God. Because she was such a good person all her life, the heavens opened to receive her when she died. This is the basis for the celebration.

As the mother of God, Mary is seen to have miraculous powers, and many people pray to her directly. There are many special dates that celebrate different events in Mary's life, but August 15th is the most important date for Greeks.

The morning begins with a church service, where everyone dresses up in their best clothes. Banners decorate the pebbled courtyards outside the church entrance. After the service, everyone goes home for a big lunch. Home-made wine is brought out for such occasions, as are elaborately prepared dishes. People make the most of the warm summer weather to eat and sit outside, and watch the world go by.

Panagia Evangelistria

The church called the Panagia Evangelistria is located on the island of Tinos. This church houses a very special icon of the Annunciation of the Archangel Gabriel, called the Megalochari [me-ga-lo-ka-RI], meaning "the Great Joy." In the Bible, the Archangel Gabriel appeared to Mary to tell her that she was to become the mother of Jesus Christ. Many Greeks believe this image of Mary has miraculous powers. Hundreds of people travel to Tinos every year, hoping to be cured or blessed. Tinos becomes especially busy during the festival of the Assumption of the Virgin Mary, when the icon is paraded through the streets, and when devout Christians crawl to the church. People light candles and place them in the sandbox near the icon, while others place precious jewelry near the icon in the hopes their prayers will be answered. Many parents travel to Tinos with their children to have them baptized in that church, believing their children will be especially blessed.

The Panagia Evangelistria is the center of the festivities on August 15th.

Left: Little girls in traditional dress with elaborate chains of golden coins. The number of golden coins indicates the girls' wealth and economic position.

Below: A beautiful Karpathian girl being fussed over by an adult in the festival celebrations.

Olympos

The Assumption celebrations at the little town of Olympos on the island of Karpathos are one of the most spectacular. In Olympos, many of the old customs have been preserved. Today, the women in Olympos still wear traditional dress daily and bake their bread in outdoor ovens.

People from all over the world flock to Olympos on the festival of the Assumption of the Virgin Mary. The village celebrations last for three days with lots of dancing, music, and feasting. Traditional instruments are played, and women wear beautiful, elaborately decorated traditional dresses. Girls wear collars of golden coins and chains to indicate their wealth and status, and to attract suitors.

Left: The town of Olympos has preserved many traditions, such as the baking of bread in outdoor ovens.

Think about this

The Greeks drink a special Greek wine on festive occasions called *retsina* [ret-SI-na]. This white wine is flavored with resin from pine trees. Many Greeks also drink this special wine at daily meals. Are there any special foods that your family eats on special occasions?

Summer holidays

August is a month of beautiful summer weather. Many Greeks take advantage of the wonderful sunshine to go camping or relax on the lovely beaches on the islands or the coasts. Some travel to the villages in which they were born to visit relatives and friends still living there. Flocks of people can be seen at the port of Piraeus in Athens as people board the ferries for the beautiful islands in the Aegean Sea. They enjoy themselves not only because it is a special time of year, but also because they are relaxed and carefree.

Below: Young people soak in the rays of the sun at the Super Paradise Beach on the island of Mikonos.

NAME DAYS

M ost Greeks celebrate their name days rather than their birthdays, the celebration of which is seen as a Western influence. Name days are celebrated on the feast day of the saint after whom a person is named at baptism. Only children celebrate birthdays in Greece. Most people stop celebrating their birthdays after the age of 12.

What's in a name?

Choosing children's names is very much dictated by family tradition. The first-born son is named after the father's father, and the first-born daughter is named after the father's mother. In the same way, the second son is named after the mother's father and the second daughter after the mother's mother. The children after that will be named after uncles and aunts who have died or who could not have children. Therefore, a person's name not only has a religious significance but has traditional importance as well.

Right: A big street party in Greece.

Left: Taking a break at a feast day celebration.

A time to celebrate

A person celebrating his or her name day may tell you, *"Giortazo simera"* [gior-TA-zo si-ME-ra], meaning "I'm celebrating today." The traditional reply to this is, *"Chronia polla"* [kro-NEE-a PO-la], meaning "Many years." The one who is celebrating normally treats friends to cakes and drinks, while guests bring little gifts.

A community celebrates

The bigger celebration, however, is for the saint to whom the day is devoted. Every town and community has a patron saint. For example, St. Dimitrios is the patron saint of Thessaloniki, and St. Nicholas is the patron saint of travelers. On such days, the entire community celebrates. There are elaborate processions and prayers to honor the saints, after which the whole community feasts and dances into the night.

Above and *below:* Elaborate processions are held on the feast days of saints, where the whole community honors their patron saint. This one was celebrated on the island of Kefallinia.

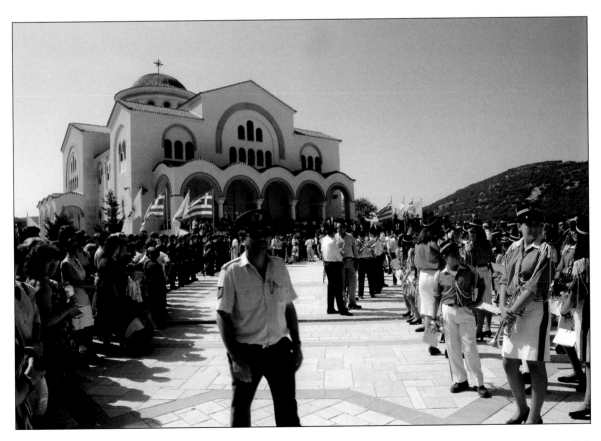

THINGS FOR YOU TO DO

T he Greek alphabet is very different from the English alphabet and has many beautiful symbols to represent letters. Today, the Greek government has **adopted** a system of **transliteration**, which guides foreigners in the pronunciation of Greek words.

A street sign with a transliteration at the bottom.

Learn to pronounce Greek!

Below are the 24 letters of the Greek alphabet. On the right of each letter is the corresponding letter in English when transliterated. The third column teaches you how to pronounce it. For example, for the first Greek letter, Αα, its corresponding English letter is A, and it is pronounced like the "a" in the word "arm." Try it!

Α α	A a	arm	Ν ν	N n	none
Β β	V v	vase	Ξ ξ	X x	axe
Γ γ	G g	young	Ο ο	O o	ox
Δ δ	D d	there	Π π	P p	pet
Ε ε	E e	egg	Ρ ρ	R r	run
Ζ ζ	Z z	zoom	Σ σ	S s	sun
Η η	I i	leave	Τ τ	T t	ten
Θ θ	Th th	thing	Υ υ	Y y	leave
Ι ι	I i	leave	Φ φ	F f	fun
Κ κ	K k	kind	Χ χ	Ch ch	look
Λ λ	L l	long	Ψ ψ	Ps ps	caps
Μ μ	M m	man	Ω ω	O o	ox

Make an Ionic column

Over 2,500 years ago, Greeks used columns to support and decorate their buildings. Greeks were famous for Doric, Ionic, and Corinthian columns, named after three Greek tribes who decorated the tops of their columns differently. You can make your own Ionic column, too!

Take a piece of cardboard measuring 10 inches x 5 inches (25 centimeters x 13 centimeters) and make 0.4 inches (1 cm) markings along its breadth. Fold the cardboard at each marking, and glue the two lengths of the cardboard together to make a fluted column. Glue an empty matchbox at each end of the column. Take a long strip of cardboard 12 inches x 2.5 inches (30 cm x 6 cm). Put a mark in the center of the strip. Tightly roll each end of the strip toward the center. Glue the middle of the cardboard strip onto the matchbox. Now you have your own Ionic column. What other kinds of columns can you make?

Things to look for in your library

Ancient Greece. (http://www.pearson.co.uk/education/catalogue/490703.html).
Athens (Cities of the World series). R. Conrad Stein (Children's Press, 1997).
Greece (Music World International series). (video).
The Greeks (Pictures of the Past series). Denise Allard (Gareth Stevens, 1997).
I Wonder Why Greeks Built Temples: And Other Questions About Ancient Greece (I Wonder Why series). Fiona MacDonald (Kingfisher Books, 1997).
Olympians: Great Gods and Goddesses of Ancient Greece. Leonard Everett Fisher (Holiday House, 1989).
Persephone and the Pomegranate: A Myth from Greece. Kris Waldherr (Dial Books for Young Readers, 1993).
Postcards from Greece. Denise Allard (Raintree/Steck Vaughn, 1997).

MAKE A CRICKET MASK

Masks and costumes are a big feature of the Carnival. The mascot of the Patrai Carnival is the cricket, a fun-loving creature that likes to sing and play. It represents celebration and joy—precisely what the Carnival is about. You can make your own cricket mask, too!

You will need:
1. A paint tray
2. Elastic band
3. A stapler
4. Staples
5. Scissors
6. Tempera paints
7. A large piece of posterboard
8. Paintbrushes
9. A black wax pencil
10. Glue
11. 2 gold pipe cleaners

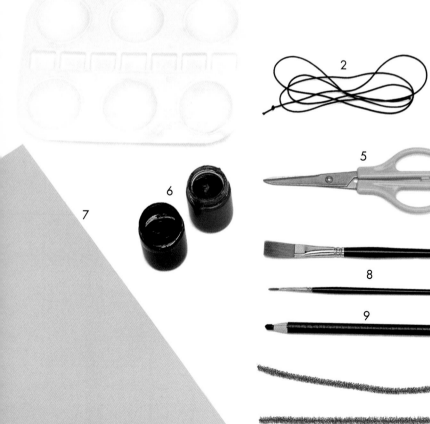

1

2

5

3

6

7

4

8

9

10

11

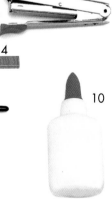

1 With the wax pencil, draw the cricket's face, eyes, nose, and mouth like in the picture above. Then draw a bow tie and hat.

2 Paint the cricket's face green. Do not paint the eyes. Paint the hat, bow tie, and eyeballs black.

3 Cut out the cricket mask. Carefully cut the cricket's eyes out.

4 Staple the elastic band at the back of the cricket's cheek—one at each cheek. Make sure the elastic band can go around your head and that it's not too loose or too tight. Finally, glue the gold pipe cleaners at the base of the hat, one at each end. Now, you're ready to celebrate!

MAKE KOULOURAKIA

B read is a very important item in the Greek menu and is served at every meal. There is an interesting variety of local bread with different flavorings, such as currants, herbs, cheese, and wild greens. Many Orthodox festivals are also celebrated with special breads. One of the most popular breads in Greece is Koulourakia [kou-lou-RA-kia], a sweet roll you can make yourself!

You will need:

1. ¾ cup (150 g) powdered sugar
2. ⅛ cup (30 ml) milk
3. A measuring cup
4. Measuring spoons
5. 2 eggs
6. ½ teaspoon vanilla extract
7. ¼ cup (50 g) sesame seeds
8. 1½ teaspoons baking powder
9. ½ cup (100 g) butter
10. ¼ teaspoon ground cinammon
11. A mixing bowl
12. A potholder
13. A non-stick baking tray
14. A sifter
15. A chopping board
16. A wooden spoon
17. A brush
18. A whisk
19. 2½ cups (500 g) plain flour

1 Whisk the butter, sugar, milk, and vanilla extract together until the mixture is light and fluffy. Beat the eggs and add three-quarters of it into the mixture, whisking well.

2 Sift the plain flour, ground cinammon, and baking powder into the mixture.

4 Place the shapes on a non-stick baking tray. Brush the remaining egg over the shapes and sprinkle sesame seeds over them.

3 Stir the mixture until a soft dough is formed. Knead the dough a little. Shape the dough into pencil-like shapes and make rings, figure-eights, or coils.

5 Get an adult to help you bake the biscuits in a moderate oven at 375°F (190°C) for 15–20 minutes, or until they are golden brown. Now you have delicious Koulourakia for a mouthwatering snack!

GLOSSARY

adopted, 26 — Chosen and followed a system, idea, or practice.
civilization, 5 — The total culture of a particular people or nation.
defiance, 9 — Open, bold resistance to opposition or authority.
exuberant, 12 — Full of life; high-spirited.
grotesque, 15 — Bizarre or ridiculous.
neutral, 11 — Not taking part in a war.
oppressors, 9 — People who rule harshly or cruelly.
pagan, 13 — Not Christian, Jewish, or Muslim; not religious.
realm, 19 — A region or area; kingdom.
repentance, 16 — Feeling of sadness and sorrow for wrongdoing.
tassels, 10 — Decorative bunches of threads or cords of equal length hanging loosely from the knot by which they are tied.
transliteration, 26 — The writing and spelling of the words and letters of one language into corresponding characters of another language.
valiantly, 10 — Bravely; with great courage.

INDEX